She's

More

Than

Christina Smith

Published By:
Jasher Press & Co.
New Bern, NC 28561
Interior PDS
Cover TJ Wallace

Copyright© 2018

ISBN: 978-1718644571

First Edition
Printed and bound in the United States of America

She's
More
Than

CONTENTS

I love Christina Smith. I love how she loves her family and friends. I love how she loves the ministry that God has called her to. I love that she can relate to almost anyone, just by being herself. I have had the privilege of being a recipient of her love and ministry for the past 9 years and am better today because of it. I know the Christina who has written the pages you are about to read and I want you to know that you will be reading truth bombs from front to back.

Christina is ALL IN. I've never seen her approach something half hearted, but rather in everything she does, she is fully engaged, open and ready to move accordingly. I know Christina puts herself out there, loving people to the point of vulnerable sacrifice. Christina is the kind of friend that every woman wants to have and the type of mentor that every woman needs. She is a student of excellence in every aspect of her life, desiring to learn more and soak up more of what God has for her... and I imagine that is why she is rooted in excellence, because she is constantly growing in truth.

As I am writing this forward, one of my greatest honors to date, I have to tell you why I love Christina so much. Simply put, she LOVES Jesus and she LOVES people. I believe the most powerful way to share your heart and passion is to pour it out on others, without restraint, and when you talk to Christina that is EXACTLY what you get. So, grab a cup of coffee, and get ready to be challenged and inspired, as you are basically sitting next to Christina as she pours words of encouragement, truth and love through the spectacular and beautiful words in this book.

I pray you read this book and discover what I have: God has given us a message of hope through Christina. And her hope, rooted in Jesus, is for such a time as this.

Angela Buck
Connections Director, Genoa Baptist Church

"She's More Than" just a friend. "She's More Than" just a mentor. "She's More Than" just a fellow pastor's wife. Christina Smith is a brave, passionate, encouraging, noble woman of God and, you guessed it, so much more! I have had the honor of witnessing a small part of her journey, and I can honestly say that she is beyond qualified to write this book.

She has walked through ups and downs with so much grace and dignity, while glorifying The Lord every step of the way. She has given me a sound example to follow in ministry and it has been pure joy to see her dream come to life through this book. Her heart has been poured out onto every page with the desire to help women realize the "something more" that God has for each and every one of us.

Logan Almore
Small Group/ Outreach Coordinator, Latitude Church

Ministry is a calling that is not always easy and not always clear in finding your place or purpose in the midst of it all. Christina Smith has set out to make it her duty to help other women in this walk, understand who they are in Christ, and understand who they are called to be. "She's More Than" takes us on a journey to understand the truths and reality of this walk, to help us find our purpose, and recognize what we may need to overcome within our selves to help further us in our walk with Him. I am proud to call Christina a dear friend and true family. I cannot wait to see how God uses this book to help other women find what they are overcomers in. Congratulations on this achievement, Sis!!

Ashley Myers
Worship Leader, Latitude Church

Kathryn Briggs "my mama"

Kathy was more than a mom, grandmother, wife, and friend.
For me she was my cheerleader, encourager, wisdom giver,
life speaker, prayer warrior, best friend and the list goes on.
We often say that the servants see the miracles. Even to the
end, mama saw miracle upon miracle displayed in people's
lives because of her obedience and servanthood. Looking
around at the family that God has blessed me with, I can see
her fingerprints and legacy that will live on throughout
generations.

I can say with every fiber in my being that she was a Proverbs
31 woman. "She is clothed with strength and dignity;
she can laugh at the days to come. She speaks with
wisdom, and faithful instruction is on her tongue.
She watches over the affairs of her household and
does not eat the bread of idleness. Her children arise
and call her blessed; her husband also, and he praises
her: Many women do noble things, but you surpass
them all. Charm is deceptive and beauty is fleeting;
but a woman who fears the Lord is to be praised.

Honor her for all that her hands have done, and let her works bring her praise at the city gates."

During the writing of this book, my mama went home to be with the Lord. She was not able to hear the last the couple of chapters nor was she able to have a copy of it in her hands but her spirit is present in every page. Just a few weeks before she passed, I was able to sit beside her and share with her the dream that God had placed inside of me through this book. I was able to read to her the first couple of chapters. I remember telling her just like you will hear me tell you that God had "something more" for her and oh did he. I dedicate my first book, "She's More Than" to my mama on Mother's Day 2018. Thank you for always loving Jesus and for loving me. Thank you for always putting others before yourself. Thank you for showing me where my help comes from. Mama, I pray that I can be half of the woman that you were and still are. I love you more than life itself.

INTRODUCTION

As we embark on this journey through ministry together, I want to first put out a disclaimer. I am in no way an expert and definitely don't have everything together. My desire is to be the best version of myself possible, and to be everything God has called and appointed me to be.

Earlier this year, I had the privilege of attending a Catalyst Conference with the staff of our church. During the entire conference, I was "all ears." I found myself hanging on every word that every speaker (expect for one, lol) spoke on. During the van ride back, we had a time of deep reflection. As a group, we shared our experiences and what God was personally speaking to our spirits. Then, the conversation turned to me. Trying to respond, I found myself struggling with some questions that maybe you can relate to.

1.   What are you calling me to be courageous in, God?

2.   What is your purpose for me, God?

3.   What is a personal goal that I have for myself?

I could answer those questions when it came to our church, but what about me as an individual? I was at a loss and had no answer. Had I lost my way through ministry, and for some reason believed that God didn't still have big plans for me as an individual? Perhaps I had lost myself somewhere in the process of starting a church, being a pastor's wife, being a mom, and the list goes on. Over the last year, I have been prayerfully crying out to God for the answers to those questions. I wanted so badly to hear from Him. I tried to find those answers in people, in my husband, in my boys, and in myself, but I was left with empty answers. So what did I do? I leaned in closer to hear His still small voice.

Over and over again, God would drop words into my spirit. At the time, I had no idea what or who they were for. I got my journal out and I began writing them down. Pondering over these questions, God spoke to me loudly during a staff small group "around the table." We had recently hired a couple of new staff members and, this particular night, they were sharing their stories. As the wives starting sharing, I could see the pain and hurt from their past, and yet they experienced God through it all. I could see their desire to be all that God had created them to be. I could see their need for community. I could see their hunger to know Him more. I could see their need to "get it right" so to speak. I felt as if I was the only person in the room. I heard the Lord speak over my life, "This is what I am calling you to - to minister, to lead, to disciple, to encourage, to come along side of staff wives."

I have to admit, I first wrestled with what God was calling me to. I remember having a dialogue in my head. Have you ever had one of those? "God, I am not qualified. I think someone else would be a better fit. Who will they think that I am trying to be? God, I don't have all of the answers. I am barely making it by myself." I felt him gently hush the nonsense that was taking place in my mind and bring me back to a point of sweet surrender. I recalled a sermon that my husband had preached a few months prior about serving. I remembered hearing him talk about how the overflow of what Jesus has done in our lives is the catalyst to share with others in service.

"GOD DOESN'T CALL THE QUALIFIED, HE QUALIFIES THE CALLED."

I recalled Romans 8:28 that says, "All things work together for good for those that are called according to His purposes."

I reminded myself that God doesn't call the qualified, He qualifies the called. With tears in my eyes, I said, "Here I am God, send me." I knew that God would reveal His perfect plan to me piece by piece, and that is exactly what He has done through this book, "She's More Than." As we dive into this together, these are the words that God dropped into my spirit to help you through ministry. I pour my heart out to you as a friend who wants nothing more than for you to be all that God has created you to be—to thrive, not just survive, in ministry. As you open the pages of this book, allow the Holy Spirit to speak to you. My prayer for you as we journey together, is that you will find encouragement, a new passion, freedom, and a pace that you can maintain for years to come.

"For we will be like a tree planted by the water
that sends out its roots by the stream.
It does not fear when heat comes;
its leaves are always green.
It has no worries in a year of drought
and never fails to bear fruit." Jeremiah 17:8

So wherever you are today, staff wife—a mom of toddlers, a pastor's wife, a career woman, a stay at home mom, or you fill in the blank, know that God has big and purposeful plans for you as a daughter of the King.

CHAPTER 1

REFERENCE POINT

"a <u>fixed</u> <u>place</u> that you use to <u>help</u> you to find your way or
to see where other <u>things</u> are"

When I think of a reference point, I think of two
questions—where did it all begin and who is our reference
point? For some of us, we tend to be defined by big
accomplishments. We tag ourselves to the roles that we play.
For me personally, I think of my reference point being the
time God called my husband and I to plant a church three
and a half years ago. It was almost like all that God had done
in my life up to that point was in vain. Was that really the
beginning? What about when he saved my life at an early age?
What about how he used me in student ministry? I realized
that I had categorized my life into sections. Maybe my life
and purpose for Christ didn't just start three and a half years
ago, but back when I was an eight year old girl and God set
eternity in my heart.

I grew up in a Christian home with two very loving
and caring parents. They not only talked to me about Jesus,
but lived it out in front of me. At the age of eight, I prayed
and asked Jesus to live in my heart. As a teenager, I tried my

17

best to "do" all the right things that any little christian girl should do. On most days I was left feeling very defeated, like I had not done enough. Looking back on my life now, I realize that I had a whole lot of religion, but not much of a relationship with Jesus. Performance overrode grace. Rules outweighed relationship. Fast forward twenty-two years, I found myself a young youth pastor's wife who desperately needed Jesus to intervene in our situation. I realized that I needed to break out from behind the bars of religion and see the real Jesus. That is exactly what happened. Jesus met me there in that moment in an intimate and real way. The good that I was trying to do had already been DONE.

Scripture tells us that "being confident of this, that he who began a good work in you will carry it on to completion until the day of Christ Jesus." Phil. 1:6

"THE GOOD THAT I WAS TRYING TO DO HAD ALREADY BEEN DONE."

He started a work in me just like he has started a work inside of you. You have value! You have gifts! You have a purpose and calling that only you can fulfill in your walk with Christ! Look

18

back over your life and mark your reference point. See where it all began for you. No matter how it happened, God promises that He makes all things new.

"Forget the former things; do not dwell on the past. See, I am doing a new thing! Now it springs up; do you not perceive it? I am making a way in the wilderness and streams in the wasteland." Isaiah 43:18-19

"Though your beginning was insignificant, Yet your end will increase greatly." Job 8:7

I am sure that your reference point may be a little different than mine. I know for me personally, seeing where God brought me and seeing His hand on my life has encouraged me to keep the course. So, what does a reference point have to do with me being a staff wife in ministry? Everything.

You see, that place that I was stuck in as a young student pastor's wife, full of heartbreak and confusion in ministry, led me to go back to my reference point in order to push through. It was hard, y'all. I am not going to lie. This was our first stop in ministry and it wasn't supposed to be like this. I remember my husband and I crying ourselves to sleep most nights. I knew that the Lord had brought us to this place, but what were we supposed to do now? I think so often, we forget where He has brought us. We get so bogged down with the mundane duties of being supportive for our husbands that we lose sight of where He is taking us. Our eyes get fixed

" OFTEN TIMES WE NEED TO LOOK BACK AND REMEMBER HIS FAITHFULNESS IN ORDER TO SEE MORE CLEARLY WHERE HE IS TAKING US.."

on all the wrong things. We get off course and stray to the right and to the left. We just determined in the scripture from Isaiah 43 that we should forget the former things and not dwell on the past, but often times we need to look back and remember His faithfulness in order to see more clearly where He is taking us.

Just recently, my family and I walked a journey of being falsely accused and misunderstood by "so called" friends. The enemy uses anything and everything to try and take our eyes off of the Lord and what He is doing around us. Did you hear me? Anything. It got kind of muddy, I'm not going to lie. I couldn't see where other things were. I started to question myself, my calling, and my position in Him. But, just like that, God stepped in and gently turned my attention towards my reference point.

As I am pinning these words to this paper, a dear friend sent me a video that she found on her phone. The video took place three and a half years ago. Talk about God's timing. The video was taken during our first meeting where my husband was going to lay out the vision of the church God was calling us to plant. After the meeting, we stayed around and had a time of worship. The song that was recorded on the video was "Greater." God you are greater. You are greater. There's no one like our God. You alone are worthy. In our times of ministry, God allows us to look back to where it all began in order to remind us of how great He really is.

I am reminded of the story of John the Baptist in Luke 1. The story begins with Zechariah, John the Baptist's father, being filled with the Holy Spirit and prophesying over his son.

He says,

"And you, my child, will be called a prophet of the Most High;

for you will go on before the Lord to prepare the way for him,

21

77

to give his people the knowledge of salvation

    through the forgiveness of their sins,

78

because of the tender mercy of our God,

    by which the rising sun will come to us from

heaven

79

to shine on those living in darkness

    and in the shadow of death,

to guide our feet into the path of peace."

    I wonder if the words that his dad spoke over him at an early age were a "reference point" for John the Baptist. Did he hold onto the words, "you my child will be called a prophet of the Most High" when things got tough and he was in prison? Did he hold onto those words, "you will prepare the way for the Lord" in ministry when people started leaving him to follow Jesus? Did he use those words to help him to redirect the people's focus to the One that was coming?

    Life in ministry is tough and it's no joke. I have learned, and am still learning, that I need to go back to the place of my reference point to sustain the pace of ministry. That place keeps me focused. Going back to that reference point is helpful for you to reflect, not to live in regret. God does not want us to live in regret. That is not His good, perfect, and pleasing will that He talks about in scripture. I am reminded of the song that says, "I don't have time to maintain those regrets when I think about the way you love me." Look back and reflect, but don't stay focused there. Don't fix your eyes on the reference point, but instead fix your eyes on the Lord.

I have always loved arrows. That actually was my first, and only tattoo, with two key words that God spoke over my life. You will hear about those words in the next chapter. An arrow is a sign of direction, force, and movement. It is used to show direction or position, a pointer. Just like an arrow has a point or dot of where it has begun, you and I all have a reference point of where it all began for us. But just like that arrow has a starting place, it moves from that point and forms a line that leads you somewhere. Take heart in knowing that this is just the beginning. Your life and mine is headed in a direction forward of an amazing destiny.

"DON'T FIX YOUR EYES ON THE REFERENCE POINT, BUT INSTEAD FIX YOUR EYES ON THE LORD."

I am so thankful that God is my reference point. He is constant, never changing, abiding in love and grace, and ever so patient with me. We need a reference point, something constant and true by which we can set our course. It is very true that your perception determines your path, and your path determines your destiny. Take care in choosing the way you will go. Your choice will have significant, eternal consequences.

"Commit to the Lord whatever you do and He will direct and establish your plans." Proverbs 16:3

Asking the Lord to direct one's path is better than having to ask Him to correct one's mistakes.

QUESTIONS TO PONDER:

1.   Describe your reference point?

2.   What path are you and your family on?

3.   Has your individual calling gotten lost? What can you
      do to reestablish that calling?

I'm More Than

_____

I'm More Than

_____

I'm More Than

_____

I'm More Than

_____

"Around the Table" Recap

It was our first Saturday morning gathering and all the staff wives were able to come, with the exception of one (thank you flu bug). I'd like to title this Saturday, "Ketchup packets." I knew going into this Saturday that I wanted to keep it real, raw, and set an atmosphere of vulnerability. Setting the table that morning, I realized I had some glass dishes, plastic cups for orange juice, coffee cups for what we all need every morning, and paper plates. Putting the food on the table, I realized that I needed ketchup for the hash brown and sausage casserole.

The problem was, I didn't have any. How do you run out of ketchup? Then, I suddenly remembered, "Oh I have ketchup packets in the refrigerator from McDonalds!" Just like that, I grabbed those packets up and put them on the table too. I couldn't ask for a better start to "She's More Than." Life is full of trying to impress and keeping up with the persona of who others think we should be. That morning was full of real people sharing real life struggles, mountain top experiences and recalling our own personal reference points gathered around the ketchup packets. What a beginning—Real, Raw, and Relevant.

CHAPTER 2

SOMETHING MORE

"the words that God spoke over my life"

Journal entry:

January 6th, 2014

"Today I want to trust God for what seems impossible. The last 6 months to a year has been a time in my personal life that I have often sat back and pondered what God is up to. What is the "more" that He wants from my family? Jason and I have felt a yearning in our spirit for "more." What that "more" is, we have no clue. We have been in a waiting period of having to trust God when we can't see the outcome.

As I read my devotion today once again, Lord, you wrote it just for me and our situation. Joshua, when facing the armies of the Amorites, had the audacity to call out to God and ask Him to make the sun stand still. And God did just that. I think a lot of times I don't have that kind of faith. Do I really believe that God can make what seems impossible in my life happen?"

29

There comes a time in your life when you are fully surrendered to God and seeking after Him with everything in you when you realize there is still "something more." For me, that time came about three and a half years ago. It was not a desire to acquire more stuff or things (Don't get me wrong, I love all the sparkles and diddles!) but I just felt a yearning in my Spirit that God had another assignment for me. I had a longing deep inside for "more" of God and "more" of ministry. I was not satisfied. I thought that I was doing a lot, and the average person probably would have agreed. But to me, God kept whispering, "I have something more."

The good ole country song says it like this:
There's gotta be something more
Gotta be more than this
I need a little less hard time
I need a little more bliss
I'm gonna take my chances
Taking a chance I might
Find what I'm looking for
There's gotta be something more.

I don't think this song got it exactly right. I wasn't necessarily looking for "more bliss" or "a little less hard time." I was searching for MORE of God and what He had for me and my family. I think we can all relate. I think we have all been there, or will get there at a point in our lives. Can you relate?

Hebrews 11:40 reminds me,
"since God had planned something better for us so that only together with us would they be made perfect."

Proverbs 16:9 says,
"In their hearts humans plan their course, but the Lord establishes their steps."

My friends and family know me well. I am the chief of planners and that has worked for me and against me a lot of times. Growing up, I knew exactly what I wanted to do with my life and was very head strong when it came to pursuing after it. As a young girl, I knew that I wanted to become a pharmacist. I worked towards that goal and got into Pharmacy school. But suddenly, I felt God shifting my plans. Up to this point in my life, no one had ever questioned my decision. Until one day, the pharmacist that I

31

was working with gave me a reality check and asked me a simple question that was life changing. He said, "Are you sure?" I remember at that moment contemplating everything and asking God if there was something else. You would think that I would have done that before this point, but nope, not at all. It was my way, my plans, my will. This was the start of seeking after God and His will. He redirected my steps to Dental Hygiene and I am forever grateful.

Ten years later, God called my husband and I into full time ministry. We were both very content and serving in our local church, but God had something more. What was God doing with me then and what did He want for my life now? During that time when God was speaking over me "something more", I wanted to know so badly what that was.

Jeremiah 20:9 says "His word was in my heart like a burning fire shut up in my bones; I was weary of holding it back, and I could not."

One might ask the question, "So what did you do?" Many people wonder how you hear from God or determine where He is leading you. For me, I leaned into God and started journaling my thoughts, my prayers, my questions, and His word. I sought Godly counsel (the key word is Godly) and I began to hear Him speak.

One way God speaks to us is through other people. I remember a particular event just like it was yesterday. My husband and I were shopping in good ole TJ Maxx, minding our own business. Right out of the blue, this man approached us and said, "I am from California and God just showed me that you are a pastor. I want to pray for you because God is calling you to something more." The man walked away and we were totally speechless. God really does speak and our faith was increased.

There was another time when my husband and I were visiting a hospital out of town. We went down to the clergy office to get a badge. Right when we were walking out, the gentleman behind the counter asked if he could give us a word that God had given Him for us. We agreed and he said that God told him my husband would be preaching to thousands one day and that God wanted us to step out in

"THE REASON IT IS A STILL SMALL VOICE IS BECAUSE HE WANTS US TO LEAN IN CLOSER TO HIM." faith. He knew nothing about us and God used him to speak right straight to our hearts.

Another way that God speaks to us is through His still

33

small voice. The reason it is a still small voice is because He wants us to lean in closer to Him. He doesn't scream. He doesn't often yell. One of the greatest ways that I've found to hear that still small voice is through prayer and fasting. Scripture tells us that some things only come through prayer and fasting. For me, it made it possible to focus and rely on God for the strength, provision, and wisdom that I needed from Him. I prayed and then paused to hear what He had to say. I do a great job of running my mouth to God, but He has so many things that He wants to communicate with me. So many of the words in this book are the words that He has spoken to me over the years in that still small voice. At the time, I had no idea what they were for or how they would all work together.

I would like to take a moment to pause and tell you about a prophet named, Elijah through a story that I have titled, "The Cave." In 1 Kings 19, Elijah was a prophet that had been busy working his heart out for the God of angel armies. Despite his efforts, the people of Israel had abandoned their covenant, destroyed the places of worship, and murdered the

"FAILURE DOESN'T MEAN DEFEAT OR AN END TO OUR MINISTRY."

prophets. Elijah had seen God move. He had witnessed miracles and God's supernatural power. But now, Elijah found himself at the end of his rope, fearful for his own life, and discouraged. He set out on a journey into the wilderness to run from God and His plans.

He then finds himself in a cave where he was taking shelter during his journey. Verse 9 says, "And the word of the Lord came to him, What are you doing here, Elijah?" The Lord wasn't through with Elijah because failure doesn't mean defeat or an end to our ministry. It was almost like God wanted him to take notice of where he was and what had happened for him to get there. He wanted to remind him that there was "something more." In verse 11, The Lord says, "Go out and stand on the mountain in the presence of the Lord, for the Lord is about to pass by." So Elijah did just that. The scripture goes on to say that a powerful wind came through, but the Lord was not in the wind. After the wind, there was an earthquake, but the Lord was not in the earthquake. After the earthquake, there was a fire, but the Lord was not in the fire. After the fire came a gentle whisper that once again asked Elijah a question. God speaks in a still small voice. The Lord went on to tell Elijah that he had a further assignment for him, "something more." I believe that God was saying, "I know you are weary, Elijah. I know that you get discouraged, Elijah. I know that you may be fearful. But, Oh Elijah, I have something more for you. You will be the catalyst in other's anointing."

> **" ... MAYBE HIS PLAN FOR YOU IS IN THE WHISPER."**

I believe we can all relate to Elijah. We all have had our cave experiences. God meets us in those moments and gives us our next assignment. God may be speaking to you, sister, and you are looking for him in the big noticeable ways. But

consider that maybe his plan for you is in the whisper.
Another way that God speaks to us is through His Word.
The Bible confirms to our spirits what God is trying to tell us.
Many times I have found myself going for runs or walks and
listening to The Word or a sermon. God's Word was always on time and it felt like the Lord had written it just for me. I love worship music as well, and God has used that in my life to speak His word to me. In the same way, God longs to speak to you and wants you to be able to clearly know His plan. That fire that

"GOD ALWAYS CALLS HIS PEOPLE TO THINGS THAT WE CAN'T ACCOMPLISH WITHOUT HIS STRENGTH."

was burning up inside of me caused me to seek after God
with everything. God began to show us exactly what that
"something more" was, and that was to plant a church and
see lives transformed for His glory. I can't say that after
hearing His voice, the rest was easy and breezy. Believe me, it
was far from that. I had to let go of a lot of fear. I recently
heard that fear isn't a sign that you are doing something bad,
it is a sign that you're doing something bold. I had to trust. I
had to surrender my will to His ways. I know that faith

doesn't always make sense, but it does make miracles. I am reminded of the passage in James where it says that faith without works is dead. We can hear God all day long. We can know what it is that He is speaking to us to change, to do, or where to go. But if we don't act upon that voice, our faith is useless. Abraham was credited as righteous. His faith was made complete when he took God at his word and acted upon what God had asked him to do. Stepping out into unknown waters was scary and it will be for you, too. But I have found in my life that some things must come to an end, so that better things can begin. I was pushed beyond by comfort zone. God stretched me like never before, which, in turn, created the deepest and most lasting growth in my life.

" SOME THINGS MUST COME TO AN END, SO THAT BETTER THINGS CAN BEGIN.."

Surrendering to Him unlocked His blessings that He intended for me and centered me in His will. So what does that look like for you? Is God speaking "something more" over your life or your family? Maybe that "something more" for you is investing in your marriage. Maybe that "something more" for you is being more intentional with your children. Maybe it is leading a group of women in a small group or living out your faith at your work. God has an assignment for your life. God always calls His people to things that we can't accomplish without His strength. The one thing that I am confident in is that Jesus always has "something more" for us. Just because you have heard Him one time and possibly acted upon His voice, doesn't mean that you can take a break, kick back, and relax. He possibly has "something more" for you. In fact, I know that He does. God doesn't just stop at something ok or something so so. He always has "Something More." "He is able to do immeasurably more than all we can ask or imagine, according to his power that is at work within us." Ephesians 3:20

QUESTIONS TO PONDER:

1.   Has God been calling you to Something More?

2.   What action steps do you need to do to hear from God more clearly and submit to His will?

3.   Who can you share with what God is placing inside of you?

I'm More Than

_____

I'm More Than

_____

I'm More Than

_____

I'm More Than

_____

CHAPTER 3

RHYTHM

"regular recurrence of elements in a system of motion"

When I think of rhythm, a few things come to my mind. Growing up, I played the piano for about 16 years. I loved playing, but I didn't enjoy the theory behind it all or when my piano teacher would get out her metronome. Recognizing notes and finding the correct keys are things we tend to pick up pretty quickly when learning to play the piano. However, one skill that many beginners will often overlook or not practice enough is keeping time and pace. To someone just starting out in music, this might not seem important, but in actuality it can really hurt your performance in the long run. Keeping the rhythm is very difficult to master. So that is the very reason my teacher would pull out a tool called the metronome. A metronome is a small device that is designed to keep a beat at a certain timing indefinitely. Metronomes also aid in a few other ways. The first thing a metronome does to improve your musical abilities is help you focus on your rhythm. It is important to know, not only the parts of a song, but how quickly or slowly to play them. The second thing a metronome is useful for is to slow down a complicated piece in order to better learn it. Finally, a metronome is a great way to practice tempos outside of your comfort zone. This helps you to improve your technique and skills. Alright, enough about metronomes, I'm about to have a panic attack.

My son plays the drums and God has gifted him greatly in this area. I don't know how he does it, to be honest. I watch in amazement of how he taps his feet to a different rhythm than his hands. The drummer is a lot of times refereed to as "the heartbeat" of the band. Recently, I sat down with my son and asked him what were some of the challenges that he faced when first starting to play drums. He said, "At first, it was difficult to learn the tempo and rhythm of the song, but once I started to listen more intently and make it a routine to zero in on the beat, it became easier and more natural." The same often goes for our lives. Whenever we are intentional and figure out our rhythm with God and ministry, things tend to flow naturally in His timing.

So what does all of this rhythm talk have to do with me, you might ask? We all strive to find balance. Women in general tend to struggle to find balance and rhythm in life, especially a life in ministry. When we finally have it figured out, something shifts and throws off the beat or rhythm. We drop the ball. Our house, car, and laundry are not all clean and tidy all at the same time. The three plates were spinning at one time, but now one has fallen and shattered. Perhaps if we stop striving to live in balance and instead live in harmony with life's natural rhythms, you and I would accomplish what matters most with less stress and guilt. So often we tend to compare ourselves to other

"…YOUR RHYTHM DOESN'T HAVE TO WORK FOR ANYBODY BUT YOU."

women and mimic how they balance and juggle life. The truth of the matter is that your rhythm doesn't have to work for anybody but you.

At the start of this year, I ordered myself a planner. I love planners. Do you hear me? I love planners! One of my goals for the new year was to get organized and simplify my life. I wanted balance. I wanted my own rhythm. I wanted what worked best for me and my family, not what worked best for my friend or fellow staff wife. I was craving something to help me slow down my schedule and life. I was craving something to help me change the tempo, so that I could better learn the people around me. I was craving something to help me practice tempos outside of my comfort zone. For me, digging deep into my natural rhythms helped me to take back control of my life and schedule.

So, let's dig deep to see what The Word has to say about rhythm and how we can relate that to our very own lives. Starting in the very beginning, Christ came in rhythm. He created everything in a systematic arrangement and pattern. There was order and preciseness. The God of rhythms has brought rhythms together. In Genesis 1, there is a call and response between God and creation. God said let there be…. and there was… and God saw that it was good. Over and over, God spoke these very words in a precise manner. The beginning of Genesis and the creation story has a rhythmic form as you read the passage, which in turn opens up a space of peace in the midst of a violent world. There is also a rhythm of six days of work, punctuated by a seventh day of rest. If God is going to start off with creation in this manner, then shouldn't you and I lean in closer to see the importance that rhythm has to play in our very own lives? It can literally make or break us in ministry. I am also reminded of the story of Samuel:

3 The boy Samuel ministered before the Lord under
Eli. In those days the word of the Lord was rare; there
were not many visions.

2 One night Eli, whose eyes were becoming so weak
that he could barely see, was lying down in his usual
place. 3 The lamp of God had not yet gone out, and
Samuel was lying down in the house of the Lord,
where the ark of God was. 4 Then the Lord called
Samuel.

Samuel answered, "Here I am." 5 And he ran to Eli
and said, "Here I am; you called me."

But Eli said, "I did not call; go back and lie down." So
he went and lay down.

6 Again the Lord called, "Samuel!" And Samuel got
up and went to Eli and said, "Here I am; you called
me."

"My son," Eli said, "I did not call; go back and lie
down."

7 Now Samuel did not yet know the Lord: The word
of the Lord had not yet been revealed to him.

8 A third time the Lord called, "Samuel!" And Samuel got up and went to Eli and said, "Here I am; you called me."

Then Eli realized that the Lord was calling the boy. 9 So Eli told Samuel, "Go and lie down, and if he calls you, say, 'Speak, Lord, for your servant is listening.'" So Samuel went and lay down in his place.

10 The Lord came and stood there, calling as at the other times, "Samuel! Samuel!"

Then Samuel said, "Speak, for your servant is listening."

11 And the Lord said to Samuel: "See, I am about to do something in Israel that will make the ears of everyone who hears about it tingle."

"SATAN CAN'T STOP GOD'S CALL ON YOUR LIFE, OR STOP GOD FROM SPEAKING TO YOU, BUT HE CAN TRY TO BREAK THE RHYTHM."

God was calling Samuel and Samuel missed the rhythm three times. Thankfully, God didn't give up on Samuel, even when he missed it. Just like the majority of us, Samuel was surrounded with someone who knew what the voice of God sounded like. The enemy came to break the rhythm in Samuel's life, just like in my life and your life, sister. Satan can't stop God's call on your life, or stop God from speaking to you, but he can try to break the rhythm. I think of my own life and the many times that I have broken the rhythm. TD Jakes once said, "There is no guarantee you can do later what you can do today. When you hesitate, you break the rhythm." Breaking the rhythm causes me confusion, brings about anxiety, leads me to comparison, and simply leads to exhaustion. Just like Samuel, God used other people to help me get back in tempo and hear the rhythm. They encouraged me, loved on me, and helped me to listen for His voice.

Speaking of breaking rhythm, my husband and I planned a trip for our twentieth wedding anniversary and we were ecstatic to get away. Like I told you previously, I feel like I am pretty organized and I take pride in being on top of things. Well, until now. One week out from our trip, I decided to go look for our passports. I knew exactly where they were and got them out of the safety deposit box. I couldn't believe my eyes. My passport was expiring the very next day. Talk about panicked! I went into a total tail spin. I called our travel agent and got the ball rolling on getting a passport expedited. I spent all day figuring out the process and spending way more money than we had planned. My rhythm went from steady and smooth, to all over the charts. I caused myself a lot of undue stress and turmoil by not being prepared.

So how would people characterize your life?

* chaotic
* busy
* exhausting
* out of rhythm
* in sync

Friend, life is full of unexpected turns and challenges. You and I have to maintain a tempo that is steady and manageable for years to come. So how do we do that and what does that look like for you? I think maintaining rhythm involves two very important practices—Engagement and Retreat.

I want you to picture yourself in a battle. For many of us, that is what we would say our lives sometimes looks and feels like. Soldiers are called to engage in the battle. As women in ministry, you and I do this all the time. We pour into people through prayer and encouragement, through compassion for others and serving others. We listen to their problems. We doctor their wounds. We counsel them over

and over again. We are front line and center. We take the
bullets over and over for others and we get injured along the
way. We are engaged in the battle. All of these things are
very good things and needed in ministry, but I think so many
times we stay in the battle and never retreat. That is when it
gets dangerous. When we never leave the battle to retreat, we
are more at risk for burn out, enemy fire, and just plain
exhaustion.

Retreat actually means to withdraw. It is a chance to
come home and tend to those things in our own lives before
God. It is a time to celebrate
the joys, grieve the losses,
shed tears, sit with questions,
feel anger, attend to
loneliness and allow God to
minister. This retreat time
enables us to return back to
the battle. Jesus's time with
His own Father was the most
important thing to him, not
his ministry to others.

" JESUS'S TIME WITH HIS OWN FATHER WAS THE MOST IMPORTANT THING TO HIM, NOT HIS MINISTRY TO OTHERS. "

In Mark 6, Jesus practiced this very thing "as was his
custom" and demonstrated to his disciples the importance of
retreat. The disciples had just performed miracles and were

51

tired. Verse 31 says, "Then, because so many people were coming and going that they did not even have a chance to eat, he said to them, Come with me by yourselves to a quiet place and get some rest." Jesus seemed to be much more concerned with them establishing rhythms that would sustain them in ministry than allowing them to be overly enamored by ministry success. Even Jesus Himself went away alone to pray. After He faced Satan in the wilderness and was tempted, He retreated to pray. After feeding the multitude, He retreated up the mountain to pray. When facing the cross, He retreated to the garden to pray.

He knew the importance of rest and replenishment in order to maintain a steady rhythm.

The Message version puts it like this: "Are you tired? Worn out? Burned out on religion? Come to me. Get away with me and you'll recover your life.

"I FOUND MYSELF NEEDING REST AND REPLENISHMENT. I NO LONGER HAD THE ENERGY TO ENGAGE IN THE BATTLE. I HAD TO RETREAT."

I'll show you how to take a real rest. Walk with me

and work with me — watch how I do it. Learn the unforced <u>rhythms of grace</u>. I won't lay anything heavy or ill-fitting on you. Keep company with me and you'll learn to live freely and lightly." Matthew 11:29-30

Recently, I walked a journey that, at the time, I wasn't prepared for. I sat in a hospital room full of monitors, computers, and tubes watching my own precious mother struggle to live. I remember being in that room at 3:30 in the morning all alone with her and suddenly feeling scared, anxious, and out of sync. My rhythm had changed. Everything that I had planned up to that point was now in the balance. The rhythm of her breathing was changing. The rhythm of her heart rate on the monitor was different. Up to that point, I had been engaged in the battle. I had been praying for a miracle and for healing. I had been making sure that my boys were going to be ok. I had been strong for my dad and brother. But I found myself needing rest and replenishment. I no longer had the energy to engage in the battle. I had to retreat. I had to allow God to minister to my soul that was hurting so badly. I had to ask Him those tough questions. I had to feel my emotions and realize that it was ok. I had to get alone with Him, cry, and pour my heart out

to Him. Later on that afternoon, I watched my mama
breathe her last breath. The heart rate stopped, and her
rhythm ceased on this side of eternity.

Psalm 91:1 says,

He who dwells in the secret place of the Most High
shall abide under the shadow of the Almighty.

I had to sit down, remain, and settle into a new
rhythm and tempo. When we remain in and settle in our
secret place, we experience the covering and protective care
of God. God met me in that intimate moment in a way that I
cannot even begin to
explain. So, as we come
to an end of this chapter,
I would encourage you,
my sister, to evaluate
your life. Take a look at
your rhythm and tempo.
Are you exhausted and
heavy laden? Come, sit at

" WHEN WE REMAIN IN AND SETTLE IN OUR SECRET PLACE, WE EXPERIENCE THE COVERING AND PROTECTIVE CARE OF GOD. "

His feet, and He will give you rest. Have you been retreating
for too long? Maybe you need to allow the Lord to pick you

up, dust you off, and get back into the battle. Whatever it looks like for you, know that our God wants to help you to maintain a regular rhythm that is healthy, manageable, and doable for many years to come.

Questions to Ponder:

1. How would other people characterize your life?

2. What are some action steps that you can put into place to maintain a rhythm that is more doable for you and your family?

3. Is your time with the Father more important to you than your ministry to others? If not.... What do you need to let go of to make this happen?

I'm More Than

_____

I'm More Than

_____

I'm More Than

_____

I'm More Than

_____

Chapter 4

SEASONS

Ecclesiastes 3:1-8

"There is a time for everything, and a season for every
activity under the heavens:

a time to be born and a time to die,

 a time to plant and a time to uproot,

a time to tear down and a time to build,

a time to weep and a time to laugh,

a time to mourn and a time to dance,

a time to scatter stones and a time to gather them,

a time to embrace and a time to refrain from
embracing,

a time to search and a time to give up,

a time to keep and a time to throw away,

a time to tear and a time to mend,

a time to be silent and a time to speak,

a time to love and a time to hate,

a time for war and a time for peace."

I grew up and currently live in North Carolina. I am definitely a southern girl true and true. Although I love traveling and visiting new places, there is just something about home. North Carolina has a lot of perks from the friendliness of people, to having the best of both worlds (mountains and beaches), and certainly their famous BBQ and sweet tea. Can I get an Amen? But, one of the biggest perks that I think of when I think of living in North Carolina, is being able to experience all four seasons. People often ask me if I like the cold weather or the hot weather

"GOD OFTEN WILL CHANGE THE SEASON OF YOUR LIFE WHEN HE IS READY TO CHANGE SOMETHING INSIDE OF YOU."

better. My come back, almost every time, is both. Just when I am getting tired of the hot weather, it is time for the fall and winter. When the winters seem long and I can't take much more of the cold, soon comes the pollen and spring. Just as seasons change in our world, seasons change in our life and ministry.

God often will change the season of your life when He is ready to change something inside of you. One thing that I have observed in ministry and in general is that this concept of seasons is hard for women to wrap their minds around. We tend to complain and compare and not live in contentment. I am at a different season in my life and ministry than I once was. The young staff wife with four small children is in a totally different season than the new cute girl that was just hired right out of school and has no children. The middle aged staff wife with aging parents is in a different season than the young woman who just recently got married and is eager to serve in every ministry at the church that she possibly can.

Though difficult as it may be, we have to recognize the season that God has us in personally and grow where he has planted us. I once heard the saying, "Stay in your own lane." Cultivate what God has planted in you. There are no benefits that come from comparing. Comparing only leads to frustration and allows our insecurities to rise to the surface. We tend to slip into complaining and quickly forget that this period of our life is only for a season.

When my two boys were babies and toddlers, I remember wishing that they could be in the next phase of development. I couldn't wait for them to sleep through the night. I couldn't hardly stand waiting for them to learn how to say mama and dada for the first time. I couldn't wait for them to walk. Now, as they are in high school and even approaching the time where they will be leaving our home and entering college, I have quickly realized how short each season truly was. If I could have one "do over" I would probably savor and enjoy each season of their life and development. I would soak up those late night feedings and rocking them to sleep. I would not get aggravated at the constant question of why. I would appreciate the mud from the ball field.

God has entrusted us to cultivate the time during each season of life to reap a huge harvest. Neglect, on the other hand, can lead to weeds for years to come. I would dare say that none of us want to deal with the weeds, but would rather be beneficiaries of a huge harvest.

Just like in our personal lives, I believe that God wants us to experience Him in each season of ministry as well, not wish it a way. Not complain our way through, but instead be content. Contentment is defined as the state of happiness and satisfaction. It is a mental or emotional state of satisfaction drawn from being at ease in one's situation, body, and mind. Paul talks about this very thing in Philippians 4:11-12. He says, "I am not saying this because I am in need, for I have learned to be content whatever the circumstances. I have learned the secret of being content in any and every situation, whether well fed or hungry, whether living in plenty or in want."

So, what is that secret? It's Jesus that gives us strength. Verse 13 says, "I can do all this through him who gives me strength." Every person who is reading this book is in a different season in their lives. Just like the verses from Ecclesiastes, there is a time for everything. Some of us

"UNDERSTANDING SEASONS SHOULD BRING CONTENTMENT, NOT COMPARISON."

are in a building season. Some of us are in a mending season. Some of us are in a silent season, and the list goes on. Understanding seasons should bring contentment, not comparison. So, what season or seasons are you in right now? Recognize the season for what it is and know that His strength will enable you to do all that is needed in this short season.

We must take things as they come to us for it is not in our power to change what is appointed for us. Recently, my small group went through the book of Esther together. I was amazed that even though I had heard this story many times, God revealed so much to me during this specific time.

Esther was an orphan who was raised by her uncle, Mordecai. The Queen died and the King was looking for someone to fill this role. Esther made sure to jump into line. She won favor with the people and eventually with the King himself. During the time (season) that Esther was "proving herself" so to speak, a guy named Haman, a counselor in the royal house who was also power hungry, issued a decree for all the Jews to be killed. The King authorized this decree, not realizing that Esther was a Jew. Word was sent to Esther about the decree and people looked to Esther to do something about it.

Mordecai sent back this answer, "Do not think that because you are in the king's house you alone of all the Jews will escape. For if you remain silent at this time, relief and deliverance for the Jews will arise from another place, but you and your father's family will perish. And who knows but that you have come to your royal position for such a time as this?"

Instead of Esther complaining, comparing, and remaining silent, she stepped into this season that God appointed just for her. She sought God's face, prayed, and fasted. Seasons, good or bad, are ways for God to capture our hearts and our faith. Through her obedience of walking into her season and knowing the perfect timing to approach the King, God used her to save the Jews and to promote her in the palace. She bloomed in the area that she was planted. She stayed in her own lane until the appointed time. She recognized that there was a time to be silent and a time to speak. She understood that there was a time for everything and a season for every activity under the heavens.

One "time" specifically that I would like to dig a little deeper into is "a time to plant." My husband and I both grew up in a farm town. Although I didn't have the honor of working on a farm (Praise Jesus, lol) I have always been intrigued by farmers and their faith. My husband worked on his grandparent's farm until he was old enough to drive away and get a job of his choice. He said some of the things that used to fascinate him as a little boy was the work that it took his grandfather to get prepared for that year's harvest. He remembers noticing how straight each row was. He remembers the little seeds that were placed in the soil. He remembers how hot the sun got in the summer and the energy it took to make it through the day. He recalls the rest that he enjoyed at the end of the day. His grandfather embraced his time of planting and, for that reason, reaped a big harvest year after year.

65

A time of planting can be divided up into three seasons. The first thing that has to take place is a "season of preparation." Farmers have to plow the field. They have to make sure that the soil is capable to handle the seed that is planted. In Mark chapter 4, it talks about this very thing with the parable of the sower. Farmers went out to sow their seeds and some were scattered among the path, some on the rocky places, and some fell among the thorns. All of these seeds were either eaten by birds, scorched by the sun, or choked out by the weeds. But the seed that fell on good soil came up and produced a crop that multiplied.

Aren't we just like this? God uses seasons in our life to prepare our hearts, to plow our figurative soil, and remove the thorns and rocks that will choke out the dreams and visions planted inside of us. I know I can fight this phase because it is painful. It takes energy and effort. But I know that God promises me that there is "a time for everything." If we miss the preparation phase and we do not welcome the gardener to cultivate our soil, we will never reap the harvest that is intended. We can choose contentment in this season.

Stephen Furtick said, "Contentment isn't just a disposition, it's a decision." God is not keeping you from it, he is preparing you for it. A seed has been planted in you and imagine what it can be. There are possibly some weeds in your soil that need some round up. Maybe you need to pray that God will help you to be content in this season. Whatever the case, know that every good thing has to be prepared. The next season of the planting process is the "season of bearing fruit." After the soil has been prepared and the seed has been planted, soon comes the production of fruit. Mark 4:8 speaks on this when it says, "Fruit that sprang

"DON'T EXPECT TO SEE WHAT YOU ARE NOT WILLING TO SOW."

up and increased; and brought forth, some thirty, and some sixty, and some an hundred." I can only imagine how it must feel to the farmers to see the fruit of their labors. It is probably similar to the feeling when we see our children serve and live for the Lord, when we see people that we have prayed for come to Christ, or when we see God move mountains on our behalf.

This is the season that we all like to be in, especially if it produces fruit that is bountiful. This season is smack dab in the middle of the preparation and the harvesting. So many things happen in the middle. If we cooperate with the processes, we will bear fruit and be productive. If we struggle with the process, we will feel anxious and frustrated. Don't expect to see what you are not willing to sow. Love, joy, peace, patience, kindness, and self control are all fruits that we have the power through the Holy Spirit to bear. This fruit will last and is definitely worth bearing. Just because we have made it through the preparation season doesn't mean that we can take a break. Bearing fruit requires us to allow the Holy Spirit to continue to prune, to continue to weed, and to continue to water. The good news is that it is not our job to produce the fruit that will last, but the Holy Spirit's job who lives inside of us. Are you bearing fruit? Have you just settled in bearing a thirty fold harvest or a hundred fold?

Once the fields have been prepared and the vines start to bear fruit, we enter the final phase. This is the "season of giving it away." This is also known as the harvesting phase. Working in the dental field, I have had some amazing patients throughout my career. I always love harvesting time around the office or church, especially if the season has produced the right amount of rain and sun. Yes, you guessed it, I was the beneficiary of lots of vegetables and fruits. They would hand me grocery bags and say, "Please take some, we have so much we can't give it away." Shouldn't that be our same attitude? God has entrusted us with so much. For many of us, we have experienced so much throughout our ministry, that the least we can do is to give it away.

My husband's grandfather recognized it wasn't just his efforts that produced a great harvest. He knew that a lot of elements had to come together to be able to enjoy the benefits of his labor. He understood that this season would soon come to an end. He wanted everyone to be able to experience the fullness of the time, so he decided to give it away. Just last year, I had to make the decision to give up working full time in my career to spend more time with my family. I also recall the time when I had to give away leading the women's ministry at my church and pass that baton on to someone else. Giving things away is vital, not only in your life and season, but also to help grow seeds that have been planted inside other women. So, what about you? What are you holding onto that you could give away?

I started this chapter in Ecclesiastes. Something interesting about the author of Ecclesiastes is that it was King David's son, Solomon, who was the wisest man alive. He recognized that there was a time for everything. Solomon used polar opposite illustrations to grab our attention. He knew that we would all be in different seasons, and that we would need encouragement. One verse that I intentionally left out in the beginning was verse 11. He said, "He has made everything beautiful in it's time." So, your season may not be beautiful right now. It may seem unfair and you may be tempted to "side eye" the lady beside you and your family in ministry. But hang tight to King Solomon's words that "IN ITS TIME" it will be beautiful.

The seasons can be harsh. The seasons can feel like a paradise. The seasons can be laborious. But learn to grow where God has planted you and embrace the process. Christine Caine once said, "We all have wilderness seasons in our lives. When we embrace the wilderness wholeheartedly, it becomes a place in which we are freed from our bondage to fear, insecurity, and disappointment. It's when we learn to live wholeheartedly, to fully embrace the adventures that come with the unexpected." So, friend, you are in this season for "Such a time as this." Embrace it, don't change it!

> **"... HANG TIGHT TO KING SOLOMON'S WORDS THAT "IN ITS TIME" IT WILL BE BEAUTIFUL."**

QUESTIONS TO PONDER:

1. Looking back over the verses from Ecclesiastes, what season or seasons are you currently in?

2. Do you find yourself comparing yourself to someone else's season? How can you learn to be content in the season that God has placed you?

3. What does the phrase "For such a time as this" mean to you in this season?

I'm More Than

_____

I'm More Than

_____

I'm More Than

_____

I'm More Than

_____

Chapter 5

LONGEVITY

"Sometimes you need to be like rubber and sometimes you need to be like a sponge." Lori McDaniel

How in the world did you survive this long in ministry? That is a question that, at different points of my life, I would have loved to sit down and ask women like Ruth Graham (Billy Graham's wife), Kay Warren (Rick Warren's wife) and Lois Evans (Dr. Tony Evan's wife). Pondering on that question, I also realize that every woman would probably have a different response and theory. So, saying that, let's pretend that we are eighty years old, at the end of our ministry so to speak, and we are sitting down together as friends with some coffee, chatting about this very topic of enduring for the long haul.

The average tenure for a pastor in ministry is 3.6 years. This one statistic is so shocking to me and saddens my heart. Failure often leads to frustration and frustration often leads to giving up. I have not arrived in age or tenure, so a lot of these principles are things that have helped me along the way. I am still in the process and I pray that some of these keys resonate with you. So, grab that coffee or coke, and let's chat.

Hebrews 12:1-2 says, "Therefore, since we are surrounded by such a great could of witnesses, let us throw off everything that hinders and the sin that so easily entangles. And let us run with perseverance the race marked out for us, fixing our eyes on Jesus, the pioneer and perfecter of faith. For the joy set before him he endured the cross, scorning its shame, and sat down at the right hand of the throne of God."

One thing I have always wanted to do is run. I would consider myself pretty active and can fast walk with the best of them, but running is a different story. I would look at those marathon runners and wonder how in the world can they make it look so easy. They aren't even winded. They appear like they are gliding across the track. I quickly learned that it was all in the training. They didn't start out one day running a marathon. There was a process. Just like me, you probably have been guilty of looking at couples in ministry and questioning how they make it look so easy. Just like the verses above, we are all surrounded by people that are cheering for us. But I find it interesting that the author does not focus on the people. Instead, he gets right to the point and instructs us to "throw off" everything that would hinder our longevity. He encourages us to persevere the race that is marked out for us. Did you hear that? Not your fellow team mates race, not the race that you did last year, but the race that you are currently in. Just like the runner that fixes his eyes on the finish line, we should likewise fix our eyes on Jesus.

I fix my eyes, but all too often fix my eyes on the wrong things. I see that fan waving, I hear that smack from my competitor, I look down instead of up, and before I know, it I am wanting to quit and throw in the towel. Paul tells us here that "for the joy set before him" even Jesus had to pace Himself and stick it out for the long haul. The joy that was set before Him was the finish line, when He would be able to sit down at the right hand of the Father and know with confidence that His work was completed. But in order to get there, He had to first endure the cross and scorn its shame. Just like for marathon runners, it takes discipline. It takes determination. It requires heart and passion. Many of you reading these words may wipe your brow right now and say, "Well I give up because I don't have discipline and determination, that's not me." So I ask you now, just like

Paul did, consider it. "Consider him who endured such opposition from sinners, so that you will not <u>grow weary and lose heart</u>" (verse 3). Consider that God that has put inside of you everything needed in order to endure. We can finish the race, and here are a few keys to help us do just that.

1.   **Spend time with God daily.** There is no possible way that you will ever reach your full potential and make it to the finish line that God has prepared for you without the empowerment of the Lord. He is your nutrients. He is the Living Water and Bread of Life. He is the fuel that it will take for you to

"IT IS NOT IN THE QUANTITY, BUT THE QUALITY OF TIME."

be able to rejoice in the valleys and on the mountain tops. I wish that I could sit here and tell you that I wake up each morning and spend hours upon hours in The Word. That would be a lie. I want to. I desire to. But the reality is that sometimes I allow my schedule to rule me, rather than me taking control of my schedule. I can tell you that the days where I have made God my priority and taken in the proper nutrients, I feel like I can run for days. Sometimes I am able to spend ten minutes. Sometimes I can spend forty-five minutes. It is not in the quantity, but the quality of time. So don't let a day go by where you don't spend time and ingest the nutrients of the Lord.

2. **Prioritize your marriage.**

Ministry in general can put stress on a marriage. Your marriage, though, is worth the investment. A healthy marriage reflects a healthy relationship with the Lord and, in turn, will result in a healthy ministry. The most important thing that you can pass onto your children or congregation might not be what you give them, but rather the marriage that you show them. All too often, we tend to put any and everything in front of our spouse. Your first ministry is your family. The truth is that God brought you and your husband together to cleave in the beginning, before the children, before ministry, and before the busyness of life. Our husbands need to hear and see us supporting them and offering words of life. Treating your husband as if he is the most important thing in your life (outside of Jesus) demonstrates to him and the world that "til death do us part" we are sticking this out for the long haul. Ecclesiastes 4:12 says, "Though one may be overpowered, two can defend themselves. A cord of three strands is not quickly broken." Longevity is possible when you and your spouse cleave and become one, and allow the Lord to be the strand that holds everything together.

3.   **Replenish and fill your bucket.**

At some point in ministry, your energy reserves will quickly run out if you are not making a conscious decision to replenish them. The cost of depletion is too high, and there is a price to pay when you allow your bucket to be empty. Depletion harms the people around you and damages your soul. Just like a car, you and I can only run on fumes but for so long before we get stranded and have to wave the white flag. It is up to us to replenish ourselves and to fill our bucket. Filling your bucket is as simple as putting those things into your life that bring satisfaction, energy, and fulfillment. Maybe for you it's going to the gym for an hour a day. Maybe it's as simple as a weekly date night with your spouse. Maybe it's a weekly nail appointment where you can sit and soak with a friend. Whatever it looks like for you, start by patching the holes of your bucket and start filling your bucket so that you can live at the top of your energy reserves. Bill Hybels once said, "You will be your best self when you live at the top of your energy bucket. You'll do God's bidding more eagerly. You'll love more effectively. And you'll leave a legacy for your family when you live your life out of a full bucket."

4.   **Tough skin and a soft heart.**

For us women, criticism can be hard and we tend to live for the approval of others. We will never last in ministry if we are led strictly by what others say about us and are controlled by their approval of us. Leaders with a thick skin are not crushed by criticism, nor destroyed by disappointing results. The pain, criticism, and challenges will tend to roll off the leader's skin without seeping into their hearts. Just like the quote at the beginning of this chapter, Lori McDaniel reminds us that sometimes we need to be like rubber and sometimes we need to be like a sponge. We need to learn when to let things bounce off and what things we need to soak up. Not only should we have a thick skin, but also a soft and tender heart. It is so important that we don't choose between the two, but demonstrate both. A leader like this loves people, but doesn't find their identity wrapped up in what they say or think about them. Nothing shows Jesus more than a woman who has a tender heart, is sensitive to others, wants the best for them, rejoices when they rejoice, and mourns when they mourn. Only by walking with Jesus can we have both a tough skin and soft heart. This, my friend, is a key that will help you to endure for the long haul.

5. **Know who is in your corner.**

One of the lessons that I have learned in ministry is that a lot of women want to be your friend, and best friend at that (lol). Not everyone is for you and has your best interests at heart. The enemy is alive and well, and he wants nothing more than to steal, kill, and destroy. I pray often that God would give me wisdom and discernment to know who to trust and who I can be vulnerable with.

"NOT EVERYONE IS FOR YOU AND HAS YOUR BEST INTERESTS AT HEART..."

There are a handful of sisters in Christ that I can let my hair down with, so to speak. I know they love me despite my flaws. They feed my soul and don't take from it constantly. They genuinely pray for me and my family and hold me accountable. This is an example of teamwork within the body of Christ. One of our core values at our church is "We can't do life alone." We need each other. Even Christ demonstrated this with his twelve disciples, and then with the inner circle, which was a select few. God calls us to guard our hearts above all else. Keeping your eyes wide open and being selective can save you from quitting in ministry when you should have kept going.

81

6.   **Seek humility.**

C.S. Lewis put it this way, "Humility is not thinking less of yourself, it is thinking of yourself less." Jesus is the best example of living a humble life. He humbly followed God's plan for His life. The Old Testament is full of warnings for those who refuse to be humble, and the New Testament is full of blessings for those who put others before themselves. By denying ourselves and looking after the interests of others, we reap benefits of being first-hand witnesses to God's glory and power. 1 Peter 5:6-7 says, "Humble yourselves, then, under God's mighty hand, so that He will lift you up in His own good time. Leave all your worries

"HAVING A TEACHABLE SPIRIT WILL TAKE YOU FARTHER THAN ANY TALENT THAT YOU HAVE."

with Him, because He cares for you."

When we humble ourselves, God's heart is turned in our direction. Having a teachable spirit will take you farther than any talent that you have. The lack of a teachable spirit will limit you to where God desires to take you. God promises us that He has got us and will take care of the future, if we just live in a humble state.

7.   **Walk in your calling.**

We talked about seasons in the previous chapter and, in essence, that goes hand in hand with the term "walk in your calling." Knowing and understanding your calling, and choosing to walk daily in that calling, will help and encourage you in the days of defeat and victory. If you are not certain of God's calling, you will most likely give up when you should push on. Don't miss the calling that God has placed on your life. If you don't live out your purpose then someone else misses out. So many of you reading this book know the calling that God has placed on your life, but instead of walking in that calling, you are sitting on your gifts and talents. We are not effective for the Kingdom of God when we are not being used up for the Kingdom. God clearly tells us in His Word to do the will of the Father. Big or small, out in front or behind the scenes, your calling is specific for you and God is using you greatly in the big scheme of things. Don't underestimate the calling that God has placed on your life. Holly Furtick once said, "Just because my job isn't visible, doesn't mean it isn't valuable. And just because my contribution isn't measurable, doesn't mean it isn't ministry."

I have found that spending time with God daily, prioritizing my marriage, replenishing by bucket, having a tough skin and soft heart, knowing who is in my corner, seeking

" HAVE THE COURAGE TO STAY WHEN IT WOULD BE EASIER TO LEAVE. "

humility, and walking in my calling are the keys that are helping me to endure ministry. There have been days that I have left out one of these keys, but I am thankful for a God that gently encourages me to keep going and to never give up. I once heard it said that if you run now, you may never stop running. Have the courage to stay when it would be easier to leave. Ministry is not for the faint of heart, but I am confident since God has called us to it, then He will guide us though it.

QUESTIONS TO PONDER:

1.   What key can you identify that you need to
      concentrate on and allow God to grow you
       in this area?

2.   What are some things that tend to fill you bucket and
      bring replenishment?

3.   Have you considered giving up?
      Write a prayer out to the Lord and ask Him to help
      you to persevere, fixing your eyes on the finish line.

I'm More Than

_____

I'm More Than

_____

I'm More Than

_____

.

I'm More Than

_____

CHAPTER 6

THE PRESSURE IS OFF

Lord,

I praise you because you have knitted me together and have appointed me to carry on your mission. You trust me and are equipping me. I don't have to prove myself, nor do I have to fit into a pre-fabricated mold. I am unique and gifted. I choose, today, to not live in fear. Help my unbelief, Lord. Allow my faith to be bigger than my fears. I inhale you and exhale the fears that want to hold me back. The audition is over and the pressure is off.

Signed, your daughter

A popular TV show that I have to admit I enjoy watching is "The Voice." The idea of the show is that people who desire to further themselves in the music industry and get a start to fame, audition on the big stage, The Voice. They perform a song with the judges' backs to them so that there is no bias in regards to their style, looks, or makeup. The judges are seated in a big, pretty cool chair that spins upon pressing a button. If the judges like what they hear and if something about the contestant catches their ear, they spin their chair and the contestant is guaranteed on one of the four judge's teams to compete to be the winner of The Voice. Nerves are flying, voices are shaking, families are pacing, but

"THE AUDITION IS OVER. THE CHAIR HAS BEEN TURNED. THERE IS NOTHING TO PROVE."

when that chair turns all pressure is released. They know that they have made it. The judge spends time with them, training them, correcting them, and teaching them to become the winner.

So many of us walk around in ministry and in life with a lot of undue pressure. This pressure is either placed on us from others, or predominately placed on us by ourselves. We act like we are on The Voice. We take the position of a contestant who is trying to prove our worth. We focus on perfection rather than the progress. We constantly live in fear. But, sister, I want to encourage you by telling you that the audition is over. The chair has been turned. There is nothing to prove.

John Piper once said, "Realism keeps you going, Perfectionism wipes you out." It's not about being perfect or

getting it right. It's about taking up your identity in Christ
and resting in that place. Recently, I was given a necklace
from a dear girl that I like to refer to as my adopted daughter.
After the passing of my mother, we noticed that there was a
common thread to a lot of cards that she would send people.
She always signed her name with the words, "In Christ." The
necklace that I was given was actually my mama's handwriting
and the words that she penned, "In Christ." I was thinking of
those words this week and it hit me that there is a difference
between resting in my identity, verses living under pressure.
It all has to do with "our position." Let me explain. I can
smile not because everything is always perfect, and not
because I have mountaintop experiences all the time, but only
because of "my position." Not a position or title that you
normally would think of, but a place that I have been
situated. I AM IN CHRIST! I am situated with Him. Not in
my circumstances, not in my past, not in my short comings,
but in who Jesus says that I am. I dwell in Him and He
dwells in me. He is the source of my life. Our position
should encourage us to take a deep breath and relax knowing
that it is not up to us.

Ephesians 2:6 says, "And God raised us up with
Christ and <u>seated</u> us with him in the heavenly realms

in Christ Jesus." We can live in a constant state of freedom because of what Christ has already done for us, rather than bondage from rules and performance. We are seated with Him. We are not pacing and full of pressure to perform, but actually seated with Him. When you and I choose to lean on God, it takes the pressure off of ourselves. It's not up to me! It's not up to you!

Pressure is actually defined as an attempt to persuade or coerce someone into doing something. It is a force exerted on or against an object by something in contact with it. We can only for a short time stand up under pressure. The pressure cooker will explode and the results can be deadly. I believe that the majority of time when we experience pressure, it is fueled by a word that haunts many of us—fear. Fear is the opposite of faith. Fear can hinder your ministry and put undue pressure on you. Fear cripples you and paralyzes you from moving forward. We live in the fear of failure. Fear begins as a thought, and if not taken captive, becomes an emotion that takes over. Proverbs 23:7 says, "What a man thinks in his heart, so he is." So, now that we know what fear is and what it can do to us and our ministry, let's concentrate on an antidote to our fear. Let's set our mind on what can actually counter act it's ugly poison.

F - Faith:

Faith is the confidence of what we hope for and the assurance of what we do not see (Hebrews 11:1). Hope bubbles up in the pressure cooker. We can be confident, not fearful. We can choose to be afraid of the threats, or we can trample over them with our faith. Three ordinary boys in the book of Daniel named Shadrach, Meshach, and Abednego could have fallen prey to fear. When asked to submit and bow to the king and his orders they decided instead to obey the one true King. The pressure was on and the fire was hot, but instead of sitting in fear they chose to stand in faith. The next time fear knocks on your door, allow that mustard seed of faith to be bigger than your fears. Recognize it for what it is worth, and know that there is hope and not despair. Choose to trust, despite what it looks like.

E - Equipped:

God has given us everything at our disposal. You have in you whatever you need to do what you were created to do. God has given us Himself and His Word. 2 Timothy 3:17 says , "So that the servant of God may be thoroughly equipped for every good work." We get nervous and anxious. We put pressure on ourselves a lot of times because we believe that we don't have what it takes to do what He has called us to do. In our own strength, we don't have what it takes. But in Christ, He has equipped and empowered us. Don't worry, you may never feel ready, but that doesn't mean that God can't use you. Fear has no leverage. There is no crack or space that God hasn't already filled in with His presence and power. The next time fear reminds you of your short comings, remember that in Christ you are more than victorious and equipped. You are more than, not less than.

A - Agreement:
In order to move past fear, we have to agree with or come in harmony with what God says in His Word. If God's Word is full of promises like "I will never leave you or forsake you", "take my yoke upon you because it is easy and light", and

" THERE IS NO CRACK OR SPACE THAT GOD HASN'T ALREADY FILLED IN WITH HIS PRESENCE AND POWER. "

"I care for you", then why is it so difficult for us to agree with those statements? An agreement has to happen in order for there to be a done deal. When we purchase a car or a house, there has to be an agreement for us to move forward

THE PRESSURE IS OFF

in the process. I am reminded of the story of Daniel in chapter 6 when he was thrown into the lion's den for defiling the king's orders to not pray to his God. How did Daniel have such courage in the face of pressure? Chapter 1 of Daniel says, "he made up in his mind." Before he was even under pressure, he made up his mind. I think this is exactly how Daniel was able to throw off the pressure and fear, because he had already come into an agreement and his mind was made up. He had faith in his God because of what he had previously witnessed. He knew that God had equipped him, he agreed with what had been written by God, and so he could rest.

R - Rest:
This concept of resting is hard, especially when you are facing fear. Resting is the last thing that you want to do when you feel pressure. "Don't stress, just breathe" is what people often tell us.

"OUR FEARS DON'T TEND TO LOOK SO BIG WHEN WE TAKE A MOMENT TO REST."

Resting is a state of mind. Fears diminish in the light of His presence. Resting allows us to look at things through the lens

93

of His perspective. Our fears don't tend to look so big when we take a moment to rest. God commands us to rest. He doesn't suggest it, but instead commands it. When we rest, we tend to take off, lay down, and change postures. Resting creates a space for God to minister and for the pressure to be released.

Exodus 33:14, "The Lord replied, my presence will go with you, and I will give you rest."

Did you catch what just happened? We made new words with the same letters that spelled fear. So, the next time that fear creeps in and puts undue pressure on you, counter act it with a faith that is equipped so that you can sit in agreement with The Word and rest. When you and I truly live like the pressure is off and operate in faith, not fear, things begin to shift. Then, our lives and the ones around us will never be the same.

"I'M MORE THAN THE PRESSURES THAT I PLACE ON MYSELF."

Peace that can only come from God begins to fall.

John 14:27-28 describes this kind of peace, it says

94

"Peace I leave with you; my peace I give you. I do not give as the world gives. Do not let your hearts be troubled and do not be afraid. You heard me say, I am going away and I am coming back to you. If you loved me, you would be glad that I am going to the Father, for the Father is greater than I. " Jesus was able to commit his spirit (his will and plans) into the hands of the Father on the cross and not succumb to the undue pressure because he trusted those hands and he knew that the Father was greater than himself. He > I. I'm more than the pressures that I place on myself. I > fear. So instead of cracking, crumbling, and cracking. You are put together. You have the means to win. You will thrive in ministry.

QUESTIONS TO PONDER:

1.   What undue pressure have you placed on yourself?

2.   Have you allowed fear to cripple you or paralyze you?

3.   The antidote to fear like we discussed is faith, equipped, agreement, and rest. Which one do you need to concentrate on and why?

I'm More Than

_____

I'm More Than

_____

I'm More Than

_____

I'm More Than

_____

THE PRESSURE IS OFF

Sometimes we need the reminder that we are "More Than." More than what we feel. More than what we have been told. More than our experiences. Start today rehearsing who you are and how God has a plan and purpose for you. I'm More Than my beginning. I have a "reference point" and there is a place for me.

I'm More Than my cave experiences. God has "something more" for me. I'm More Than the chaos that surrounds me. I am maintaining a "rhythm" that will sustain me. I'm More Than the opinions of others. I am

"START TODAY REHEARSING WHO YOU ARE AND HOW GOD HAS A PLAN AND PURPOSE FOR YOU."

in a "season" where God is cultivating something inside of me. I'm More Than confident. I choose to fix my eyes on Jesus and no one can steal my "longevity." I'm More Than my fears. I have faith that is equipped and I can sit in agreement with His word and rest. "The pressure is off."

My prayer is that you will use the things that God has challenged you with through this book to pour into someone else. Don't allow it to stop here. Allow this to be a catalyst to step outside of your comfort zone and be courageous!

98

Love like Jesus, lead by example, mentor your fellow sister, and grow and cultivate relationships. Together we will not just survive but thrive in ministry!

She's
More
Than

Christina Smith